HAL•LEONARD

JAZZ PLAY-ALONG®

Book and CD for B♭, E♭, C and Bass Clef Instruments

volume 139

BOOK

CD

Arranged and Produced by
Mark Taylor and Jim Roberts

Cover photo © Photofest

ISBN 978-1-4234-9454-6

HAL•LEONARD®
CORPORATION

7777 W. BLUEMOUND RD. P.O. BOX 13819 MILWAUKEE, WI 53213

Visit Hal Leonard Online at
www.halleonard.com

JULIAN "CANNONBALL" ADDERLEY

Volume 139

Arranged and Produced by
Mark Taylor and Jim Roberts

Featured Players:

John Desalme–Sax
Tony Nalker–Piano
Jim Roberts–Bass
Todd Harrison–Drums

Recorded at Bias Studios, Springfield, Virginia
Bob Dawson, Engineer

HOW TO USE THE CD:

Each song has <u>two</u> tracks:

1) Split Track/Melody

Woodwind, Brass, Keyboard, and **Mallet Players** can use this track as a learning tool for melody style and inflection.

Bass Players can learn and perform with this track – remove the recorded bass track by turning down the volume on the LEFT channel.

Keyboard and **Guitar Players** can learn and perform with this track – remove the recorded piano part by turning down the volume on the RIGHT channel.

2) Full Stereo Track

Soloists or **Groups** can learn and perform with this accompaniment track with the RHYTHM SECTION only.

CANNONBALL

BY JOSEF ZAWINUL

DOMINATION

CD

◆3: SPLIT TRACK/MELODY
◆4: FULL STEREO TRACK

C VERSION

BY JULIAN ADDERLEY

IF THIS ISN'T LOVE

WORDS BY E.Y. "YIP" HARBURG
MUSIC BY BURTON LANE

C VERSION

FIDDLER ON THE ROOF

CD

5 : SPLIT TRACK/MELODY
6 : FULL STEREO TRACK

C VERSION

I'M GLAD THERE IS YOU
(IN THIS WORLD OF ORDINARY PEOPLE)

WORDS AND MUSIC BY PAUL MADEIRA
AND JIMMY DORSEY

C VERSION

Jeannine

BY DUKE PEARSON

CD
1 : SPLIT TRACK/MELODY
2 : FULL STEREO TRACK

C VERSION

MEDIUM SWING

JOYCE'S SAMBA

BY DURVAL FERREIRA
AND MAURICIO EINHORN

CD

⏺ : SPLIT TRACK/MELODY
⏺ : FULL STEREO TRACK

C VERSION

MEDIUM BOSSA

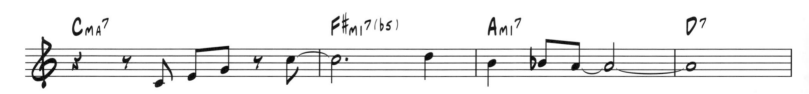

SACK OF WOE

BY JULIAN ADDERLEY

C VERSION

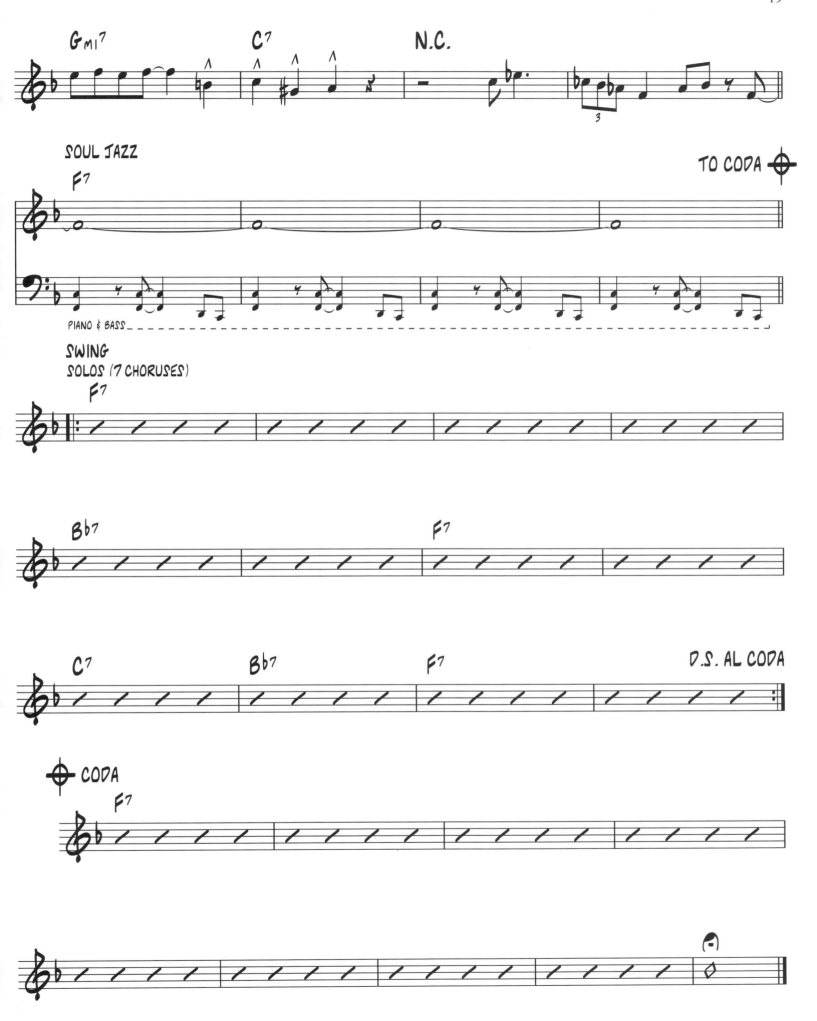

YOU GOT IT

BY JULIAN "CANNONBALL" ADDERLEY

C VERSION

MEDIUM SWING

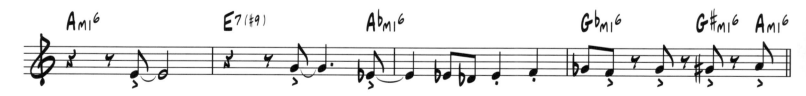

PORKY

BY JULIAN ADDERLEY
AND NAT ADDERLEY

PORKY

BY JULIAN ADDERLEY
AND NAT ADDERLEY

CANNONBALL

BY JOSEF ZAWINUL

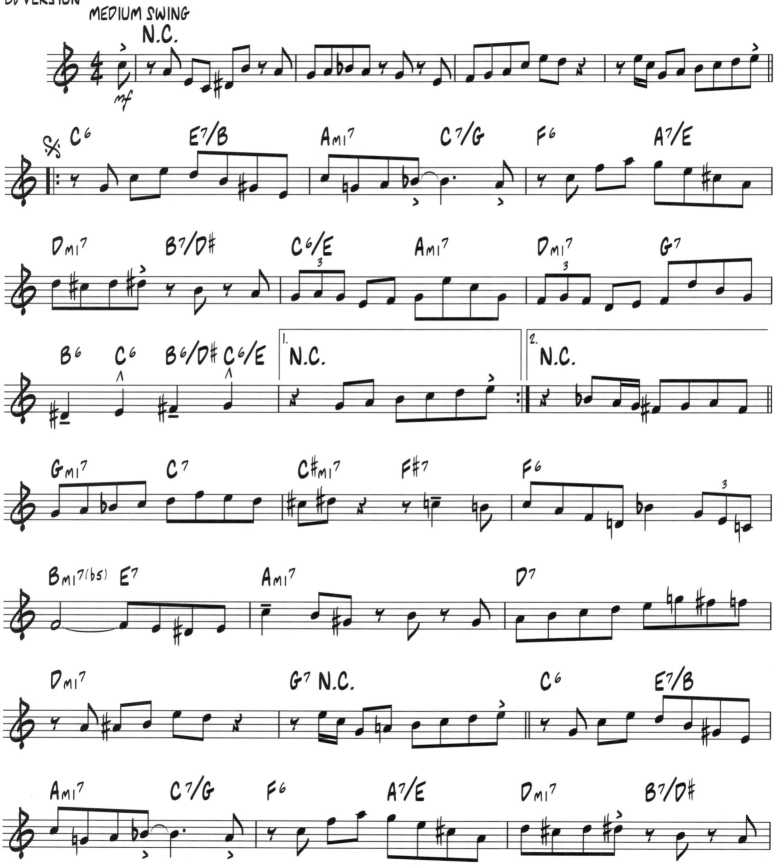

DOMINATION

CD
- 3 : SPLIT TRACK/MELODY
- 4 : FULL STEREO TRACK

BY JULIAN ADDERLEY

Bb VERSION

If This Isn't Love

WORDS BY E.Y. "YIP" HARBURG
MUSIC BY BURTON LANE

CD
◆ 9 : SPLIT TRACK/MELODY
◆ 10 : FULL STEREO TRACK

Bb VERSION   FAST SWING

FIDDLER ON THE ROOF

WORDS BY SHELDON HARNICK
MUSIC BY JERRY BOCK

CD

⑤ : SPLIT TRACK/MELODY
⑥ : FULL STEREO TRACK

Bb VERSION

CD

I'M GLAD THERE IS YOU
(IN THIS WORLD OF ORDINARY PEOPLE)

WORDS AND MUSIC BY PAUL MADEIRA
AND JIMMY DORSEY

Bb VERSION

Jeannine

BY Duke Pearson

Bb VERSION

Joyce's Samba

BY DURVAL FERREIRA
AND MAURICIO EINHORN

SACK OF WOE

BY JULIAN ADDERLEY

CD

17 : SPLIT TRACK/MELODY

18 : FULL STEREO TRACK

Bb VERSION

YOU GOT IT

CD

19 : SPLIT TRACK/MELODY
20 : FULL STEREO TRACK

BY JULIAN "CANNONBALL" ADDERLEY

Bb VERSION

41

CANNONBALL

BY JOSEF ZAWINUL

DOMINATION

BY JULIAN ADDERLEY

CD

❸ : SPLIT TRACK/MELODY
❹ : FULL STEREO TRACK

Eb VERSION

If This Isn't Love

WORDS BY E.Y. "YIP" HARBURG
MUSIC BY BURTON LANE

FIDDLER ON THE ROOF

WORDS BY SHELDON HARNICK
MUSIC BY JERRY BOCK

CD

5 : SPLIT TRACK/MELODY
6 : FULL STEREO TRACK

Eb VERSION

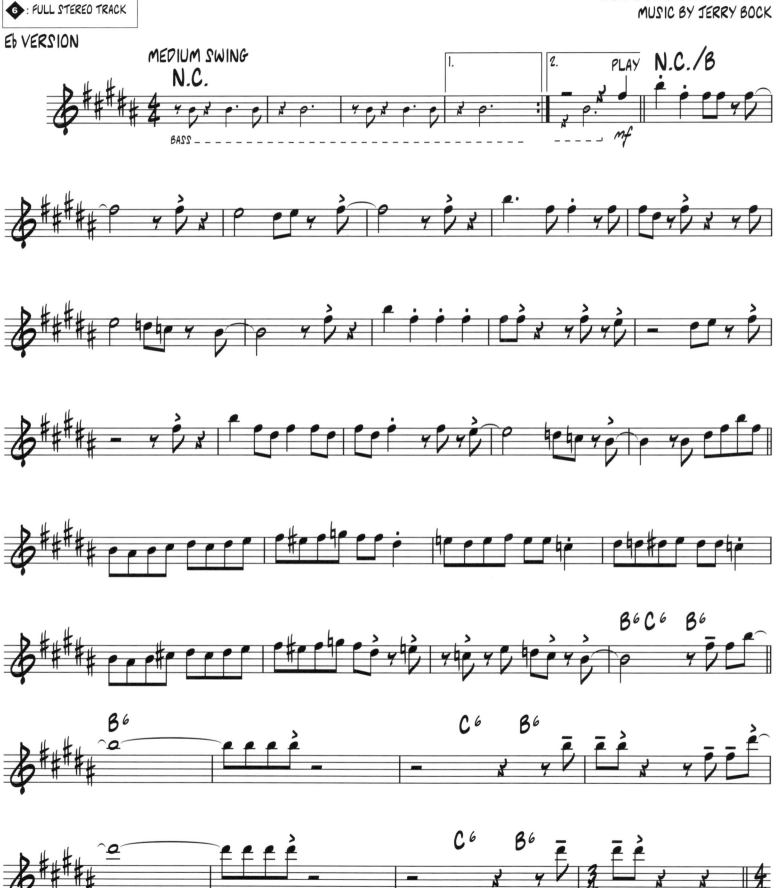

CD
7 : SPLIT TRACK/MELODY
8 : FULL STEREO TRACK

I'M GLAD THERE IS YOU
(IN THIS WORLD OF ORDINARY PEOPLE)

WORDS AND MUSIC BY PAUL MADEIRA
AND JIMMY DORSEY

Eb VERSION

CD
11 : SPLIT TRACK/MELODY
12 : FULL STEREO TRACK

JEANNINE

BY DUKE PEARSON

Eb VERSION

Joyce's Samba

BY DURVAL FERREIRA
AND MAURICIO EINHORN

CD
- 13 : SPLIT TRACK/MELODY
- 14 : FULL STEREO TRACK

Eb VERSION

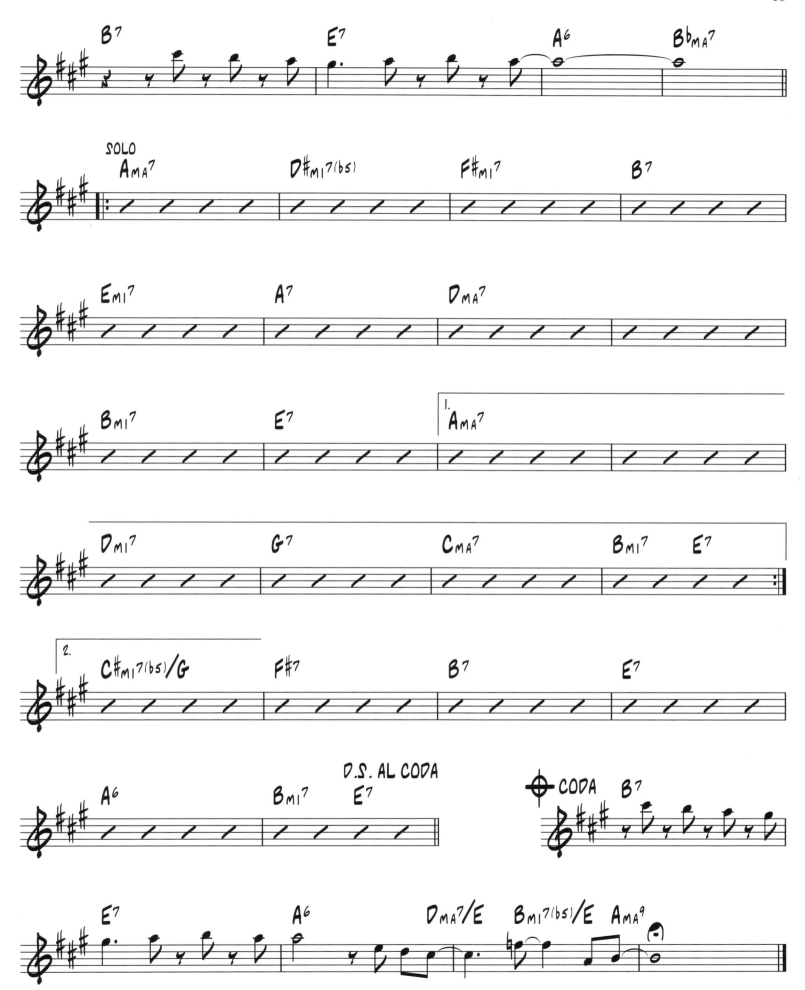

SACK OF WOE

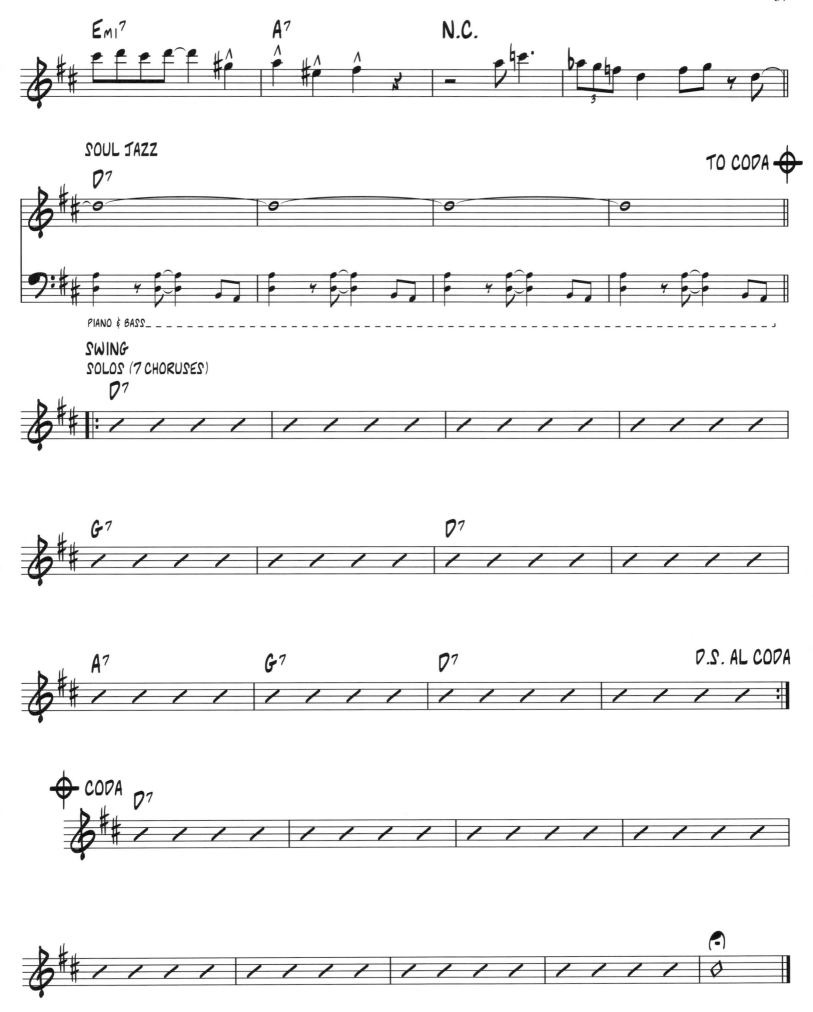

CD

19 : SPLIT TRACK/MELODY
20 : FULL STEREO TRACK

YOU GOT IT

BY JULIAN "CANNONBALL" ADDERLEY

Eb VERSION

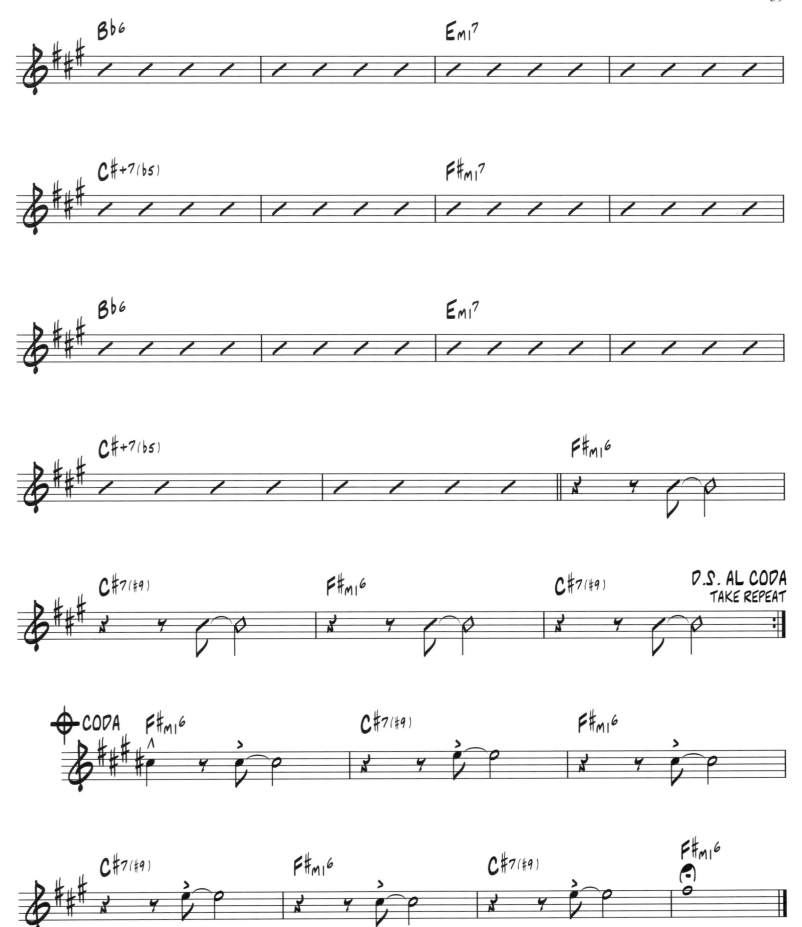

PORKY

CD
◆15 : SPLIT TRACK/MELODY
◆16 : FULL STEREO TRACK

BY JULIAN ADDERLEY
AND NAT ADDERLEY

Eb VERSION

PORKY

BY JULIAN ADDERLEY
AND NAT ADDERLEY

CD
◆15: SPLIT TRACK/MELODY
◆16: FULL STEREO TRACK

𝄢: C VERSION

CANNONBALL

BY JOSEF ZAWINUL

𝄢: C VERSION

DOMINATION

BY JULIAN ADDERLEY

♭: C VERSION

FAST MODAL JAZZ

SOLOS (PLAY 46 X'S)

D.C. AL CODA

If This Isn't Love

CD
◆ 9 : SPLIT TRACK/MELODY
◆ 10 : FULL STEREO TRACK

WORDS BY E.Y. "YIP" HARBURG
MUSIC BY BURTON LANE

𝄢: C VERSION FAST SWING

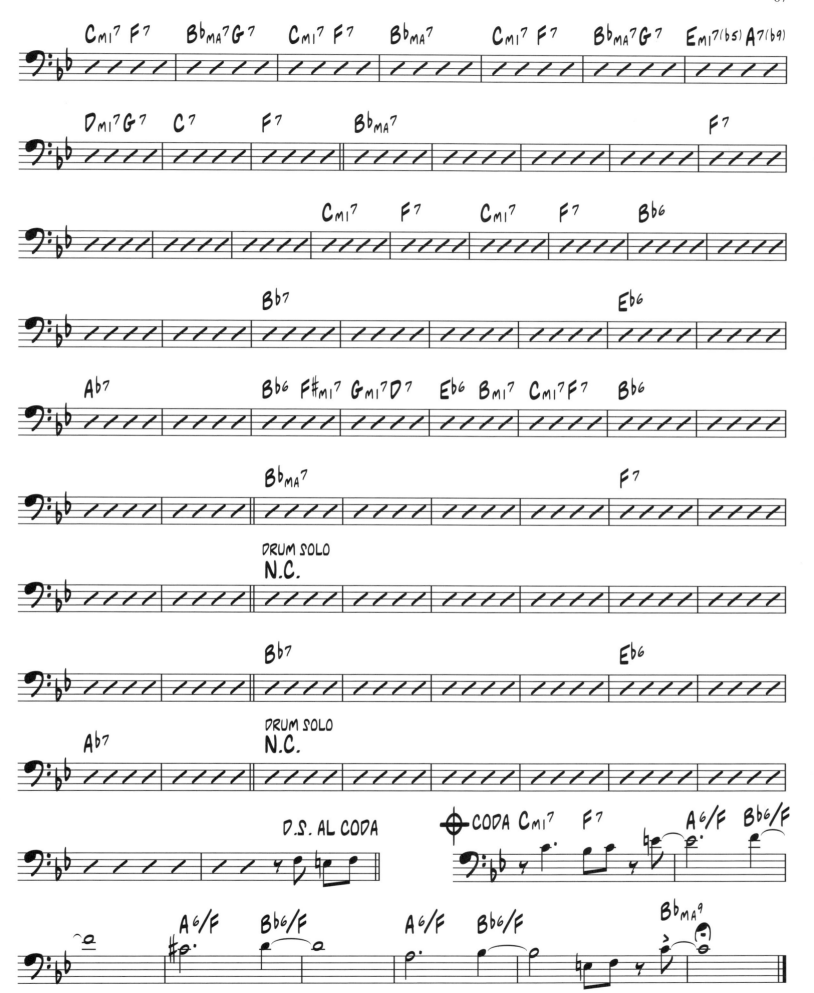

FIDDLER ON THE ROOF

WORDS BY SHELDON HARNICK
MUSIC BY JERRY BOCK

5 : SPLIT TRACK/MELODY
6 : FULL STEREO TRACK

𝄢: C VERSION

I'M GLAD THERE IS YOU
(IN THIS WORLD OF ORDINARY PEOPLE)

WORDS AND MUSIC BY PAUL MADEIRA
AND JIMMY DORSEY

CD

11 : SPLIT TRACK/MELODY
12 : FULL STEREO TRACK

Jeannine

BY DUKE PEARSON

𝄢: C VERSION

CD
13 : SPLIT TRACK/MELODY
14 : FULL STEREO TRACK

JOYCE'S SAMBA

BY DURVAL FERREIRA
AND MAURICIO EINHORN

𝄢: C VERSION

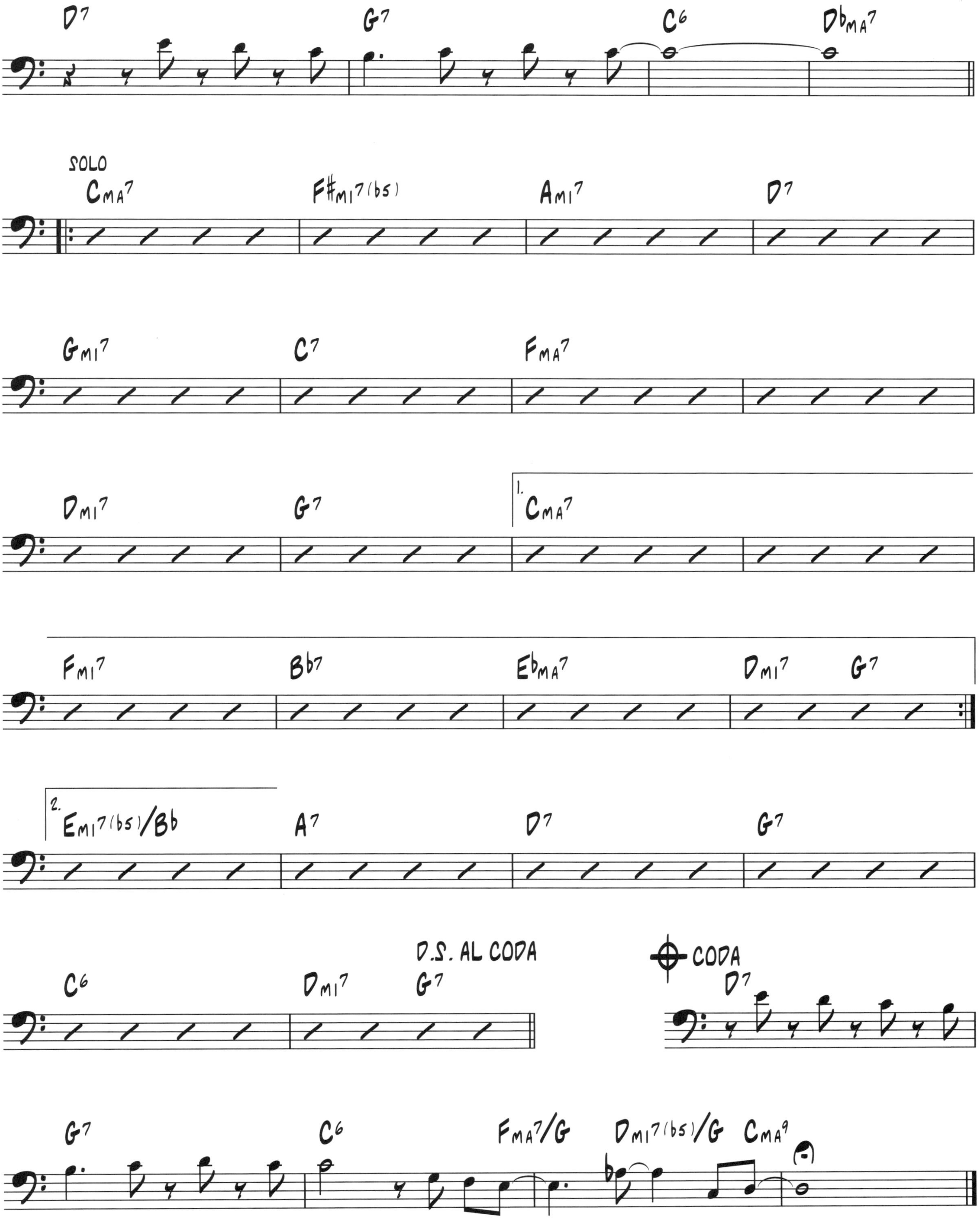

D7
G7
C6
DbMA7
SOLO
CMA7
F#MI7(b5)
AMI7
D7
GMI7
C7
FMA7
DMI7
G7
1.
CMA7
FMI7
Bb7
EbMA7
DMI7
G7
2.
EMI7(b5)/Bb
A7
D7
G7
D.S. AL CODA
C6
DMI7
G7
CODA
D7
G7
C6
FMA7/G
DMI7(b5)/G
CMA9

CD

SACK OF WOE

BY JULIAN ADDERLEY

𝄢 C VERSION

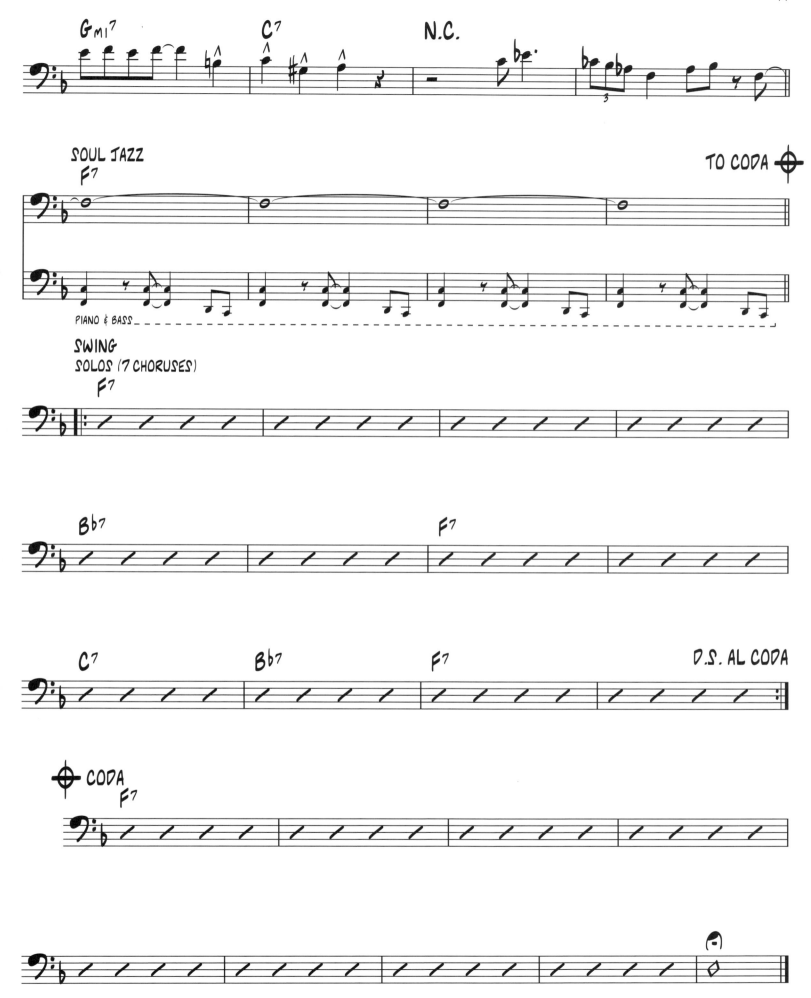

CD

19: SPLIT TRACK/MELODY
20: FULL STEREO TRACK

YOU GOT IT

BY JULIAN "CANNONBALL" ADDERLEY

𝄢: C VERSION